Incandescent Mind
Authors & Artists

Adrian Cepeda	25
Aja Beech	65
Alexis Rhone Fancher	20
Amanda Martin	69
Amanda Mathews	15, 30
Andrew Brown	42
Anna Szilagyi	35
A. Riding	36, 55, 66
Boris Ingles	23, 32
Brandi Conder	6
Brandon Dumais	62
Cat Brendel	11
Daniel McGinn	31
Darcy Smith	9
Donald Illich	32
E. Amato	3
Ed Baines	64
E. Laura Golberg	4
Elder Zamora	3
Ellen Stone	48
Erika Ayón	22
Garrett Hoffman	53
Jackie Joice	26, 41
Jane Roe	18
John Guzlowski	20
Joy Shannon	53, 56, 70
K. Andrew Turner	51
Kara Dennison	67
Ken Oddist Jones	7
Kerfe Roig	29
Kevin Ridgeway	62
Kim Sharp	68
Kit Courter	69
Kristina England	55
Laura Langston	54
Laura Saint Martin	51
Leah Mueller	38
Lynn Azali	5
Lynne Viti	65
Mariano Zaro	45
Mark Smith-Soto	33
Mary McCarthy	57
Michael Cantin	43
Michele Rene	8, 34, 47
Nancy Correro	41
Natalie Hirt	21
Natalie Morales	4
Nina Bannett	27
Nina Johnson	24
Ola Faleti	59
Ricardo Vidana	2, 44, 58
Robert Hoffman	57
Robin Axworthy	16
Roopa Dudley	61
Sander Roscoe Wolff	12
Sarah A. Davis	19
Sarah Lim	48
Serena Solin	58
Sharon Elliott	9
Stephanie Barbé Hammer	60
Stephen Linsteadt	50
Steve Lossing	63
Susan Solomon	52
Taylor Flynn	46
TC Boyd	12
Tim Perez	10
Tobi Alfier	28
Tony Gloeggler	10
Torrin Greathouse	52
Victoria Griffin	42
Yeggi Kaela Watts	17

Further information about all of our authors and artists can be found at SadieGirlPress.com.

Inside

Ricardo Vidana

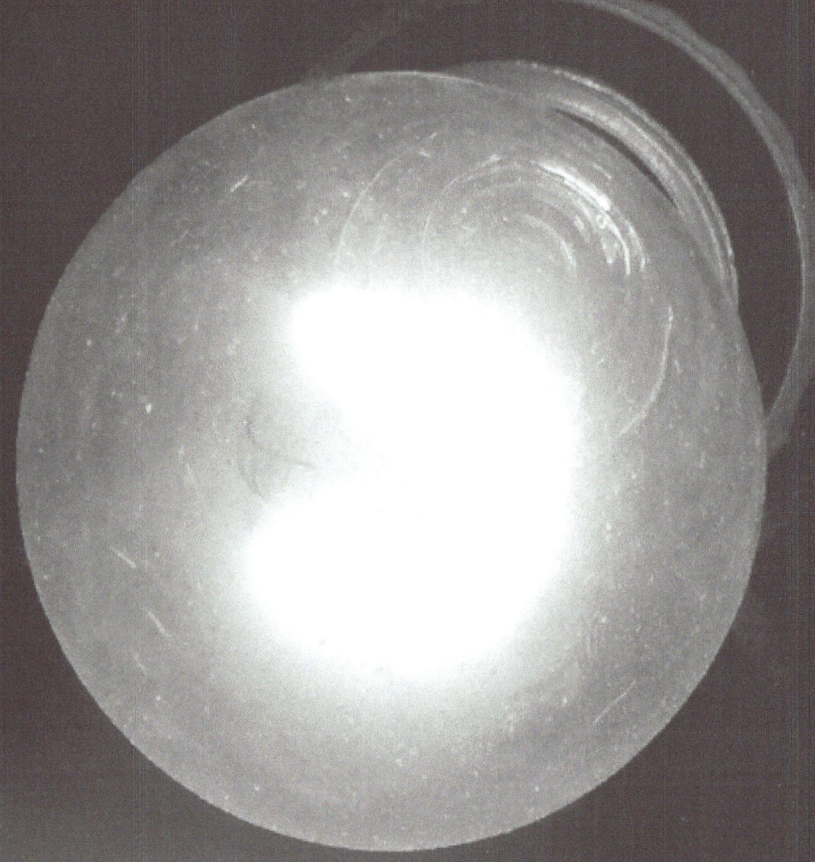

Incandescent Mind: Issue One, Summer 2016
Chief Editor: Sarah Thursday, Assistant Editor: Raquel Reyes-Lopez
Selection Committee: Clifton Snider, Frank Kearns, Jeri Thompson, Karie McNeley, Raquel Reyes-Lopez, and Sarah Thursday
Layout and Design: Sarah Thursday
Proofreading and Editing Assistance: Frank Kearns, Jeri Tompson, and Robin Axworthy
Cover Art: "Filament" by Ricardo Vidana
Copyright 2016 Sadie Girl Press
Long Beach, California
ISBN-10:0-9978155-0-7
ISBN-13:978-0-9978155-0-4
The following pieces have been previously published:
John Guzlowski, "My Father's Prayer" in *Echoes of Tattered Tongues*
Leah Mueller, "Texas Midlife Crisis" in *Crab Fat Magazine*
Tobi Alfier, "The Artist" in *Other Voices Poetry*
Tony Gloeggler, "Magnitude" in *Columbia Poetry Review*

PTSD

I invite you to stay
if you feel you need
as long as you are self-aware.

I invite you to leave
if you feel you are ready
and your work is done.

I shall remark on neither
as long as you fully stay
or fully leave.

Please
just don't stand in the entryway
blocking everything in your path
trying to come and go.

C. Amato

Elder Zamora

Figure Study 1 in Purple

Natalie Morales

Beginner's Guide to Depression

  Keep the pain at bay for as long as possible. Wrap it up, knock it out, tippy-toe around it, shimmy-shake beside it. It's not a tulip, it's a spaceship; it's not a thick cock, it's a dull rock. Whatever you think it is, it isn't, but someday it will be. You probably would have died young if not for those baby aspirin. Shit, maybe you did die.

  When it starts seeping through, as all liquids are wont to do, plug yourself up with Play-Doh. Find the cracks and go from there. Listen to me, now: whatever you do, don't sneeze. When the night feels suffocating, think of daytime. When the day's too bright, go inside. Light a lamp, for Christ's sake. Keep warm, but don't smother yourself in the blankets.

  There's nothing you can do to stop the world from turning. Now that fevers don't kill us, we think we're invincible, but we're all going to die and you'd better get used to it. We think we're better than nature, but look at your hairy legs at your post-webbed toes: we're still animals, fish, and when your mom told you that you were special, she was drunk off mini-vodka bottles. Fear isn't really fear until you're afraid.

  Ignore the pain. Hide it. No one has to know. Spread a smile across your face like peanut butter on toast. It's sticky; you'll get used to it. Embrace the anxiety. Get drunk on Saturdays and howl at the moon. Just don't tell your therapist; she'll use her no-longer-webbed fingers to write you a prescription for blindfolds.

  Now, how would you feel if I told you there's more of us?

E. Laura Golberg

Lesson
for Dr. D

I left my mind
    crushed and shattered,
    glass on a road

after an accident,
    beads of evidence
    chaining necklace of loss—

I was empty as a well
    in California, stones rattling
    all the way down.

"I wrote poetry,"
    I tell the doctor.
    "Now I can't read it, or write."

Prescription:
    "Bring in a poem you love,
    we'll discuss it tomorrow."

I open my Elizabeth Bishop,
    Too much losing in *One Art*,
    Lose something every day.

I bring in *The Moose*.
    I pause in the reading—
    a loose plank rattles

but doesn't give way.

Lynn Azali
untitled

Brandi Conder

Dogs of War

Shakespeare wrote "cry havoc and let slip the dogs of war".
Yes, let's.
I have unleashed the brain beast. My husband asks casually
every few nights, "Have you taken your pills?"
In every way, I am honest with him,
but here, I harbor my lies.
Yes, I insist I have taken the nasty things.
I would swear in court on a stack of bibles,
but here it is, my coming out party.
Bipolar and beautiful.
Just my little nod to candy coating.
Frequently non-compliant.
They'll tell you most mental patients are.
We like to know we are alive still
beneath the outer wrappings of placid complacency.
This is what the drugs do. They keep you alive enough to know
you are mostly dead.
When I am "well" I miss the fire that warms my hands
illuminates my eyes and then turns wild to burn my house down
with everyone I love trapped inside.
Well, maybe not that last bit.
I've moved on from finding fulfillment in infernos, but
the rest of it is true.
Mania is why we put the pills away and cancel
appointments with therapists and the pimps of psychiatry.
It feels so good to burn. This is the sacred flame of godhood.
I am in touch with every life in the universe.
Language at the speed of light. I hear colors. I taste words.
I love everyone, even for a rare moment, myself.
No daddy issues, no body warping. No pain. No doubt.
I am an arrow in flight. I am nuclear. I am supernova.
I see connections in everything. I can't reach a fast enough speed.
My ears roar for sound in ever increasing decibels.
No pleasure on earth has the power of mania.
If only I could live here, but fire needs fuel
and you are feeding it your life.
My husband knows what comes next.
We have lived together through the aftermath many times
and the story never changes.
When the fire burns out, all is char
and it crumbles at a whisper.
Suicide sounds so sexy suddenly.
Was it Odysseus who lashed himself to the mast
so he could hear the alluring sirens without succumbing?
Did he achieve balance then?
Will I?
I tell no one except when I tell you all at once.
I cannot live in a bottle of pills
and let its label define all the territory of my life
and yet I know no one can stand next to a fire starter for long.

Ken Oddist Jones *Holy Sisters*

I would not put my husband, my daughter or mother
through another round of visiting hours at the crisis unit.
That's where they put us once the fire is gone
till we can gather fresh fuel and fuses.
Till the drugs anesthize us into lambs in the slaughter line.
Once, we were shamans. Once, we were poets.
Now we are problems and medical bills and people cows
who need to be asked "did you take your pills tonight?"
Dogs of war. I am one.

Michele Rene
Heart Felt II

Sharon Elliott

Sea Glass
for my daughter, who died

this is my year of living dangerously
broken heart
on the edge of a broken mind
the other side of mystery

when I think I am safe
talking with a friend
trading stanzas with a kind poet
peaceful
clear eyed
whole

it comes rolling back
dancing
on a curtain of tears
it is real
there is no changing

what has walked away
will not return
what has let go
will not embrace me again
except in dreams
and memories

open-chested
broken
unbowed
I contemplate
the possibility
of picking pieces of sea glass
from the sand
the color of her eyes

Darcy Smith

No Words

Daring blue skies glare down the oak
covered path that snakes to her house.

I step over leaves the size of hands,
cross hatched, damp from rain pounding.

It's not autumn yet, but they fell
their secrets piled there, impossible

to ask what it feels like
to be flung to the ground.

I sit Shiva with a mother, an hour
a lifetime, a daughter gone.

Mirrors covered, her girl's picture propped
on a cold woodstove, lone candle stutters.

Clusters of women sit, crying in her living room
one whispers, "I don't know how to help her."

Someone stands, sings a quivering acapella
"There ought to be a lullaby for grown-ups".

On the 15-year-old's shrine, a hard wood puzzle,
each pastel letter of her name rests in its place.

The young oaks silent, her daughter slipped
into the soft light of that sudden morning.

She picked a tree. And leapt.
Her secrets piled there, impossible

to ask what it feels like
to be flung to the ground.

Tony Gloeggler

a tree with green branches

i watch the boy reach out: hands
spastic gripping, squeezing the air
thin. his father presses his hands
down and they rise, hands jerking
signing in tongues, waving
like a preacher invoking the lord.
his father grabs at his son's hands
that flit across the table fingers
become birds startled to flight;
he grips them, pushes them to the table;
they squirm and dance across it like netted
fish. the father says, "breathe michael
breathe" and the boy groans as if possessed
and the father raises his son's hands
to his face and the boy runs his hands
down the sides of his father's skull
memorizing the indentations, the minute
scars, the tracks of dry tears like small
birds; after a few moments the father
places his son's hands on his shoulders
and the father places his hands on his
son's shoulders and they both rise—
as if being pulled by strings attached
to the top of their heads—they meet
in the middle of the table bowing head
to head the father whispering some silent
prayer the boy breathing through his mouth
like a wild horse like something tamed
like something loved. the boy's chest, once
heaving, rises and falls gently as the sea
within calms to a silent ebb.

Tim Perez

Magnitutde

My friend's wife has a niece
who is autistic. He doesn't seem
to believe that I never wish
Jesse was different. He talks
about missing the big things
like proms and graduations.
I joke about the perks, not
worrying about Jesse using
nonprescription drugs, driving
drunk on weekends, paying
for college, pretending to like
the woman he wants to marry.
I tell him I take Jesse as he is
and I know what not to expect,
how every new tiny thing
he does grows in magnitude:
the first time he ran to me, grabbed
my hand when I picked him up
at school, the first morning
he walked into our Brooklyn
bedroom to cuddle between us,
that one time he scavenged
through his cluttered sensations,
strung four words together
and told me clearly 'Tony
come back August.' I explain
I am one of the chosen few
that Jesse invites into his world
and it helps me imagine
I am special with unique super
powers. But yes, I am lying
a bit. I've always wanted to lift
him on my shoulders, six years
old and singing that he believes
in the promise land at a Springsteen
show, play some one-on-one
in a schoolyard, keeping it
close and never letting him
win until he beat me on his own.
And yes, this past weekend
in Vermont, I wish he watched
television. We would have sat
and argued when Girardi
benched A-Rod, ate salty snacks
as the Yanks played the Orioles
in the deciding fifth game.
Instead, I sat on a kitchen stool,
listening to the radio broadcast
while Jesse was happy in his room
tearing pages of picture books
into piles of thin paper strips.

Cat Brendel

Head Graffiti: Nature's Dance

My Father's Shadow

He kept asking me over and over who I went out with, where we went. Maybe not the smartest thing I've ever done, but I lost it and screamed, "I've already told you fifty times you drunk, deaf bastard!" The words spilled out, a puddle on the floor I would never be quick enough to lay a towel over.

My father was offended, a taunted animal in a cage, pacing, waiting for the smallest sign of weakness or distraction to surge into attack. I saw his eyes. I saw them soften before blazing fire, his very humanity wounded. I saw his heart beat a fraction slower. His feelings of worthlessness confronted his actual worthlessness. I was hammering at his dreams, his illusions of brilliance, of superiority, of being loved. I had removed his artifice and armor.

And then I saw it disappear. His humanity and his worthlessness dove deep within. The fire in his eyes overtook him, engulfed him. A fire that determined I was the oxygen - and he leapt. He stopped in the middle to tell me he loves me and Mom. I iterated a simple fact. "She doesn't love you anymore." The amygdala gained full control. He meant to eradicate the pain, eradicate me.

He didn't. Not completely. I didn't know that other people didn't feel it, too. The forgetfulness, the walking into walls, the odd moods. But mostly, learning that words come when I give them pen and paper. I write in the hope that the friction of the pen on the page will slow the voices that freeze my already listless mind. Something, anything, to give them room to move, their words cast loose without filter or judgement.

Ego-states. That's the term I've become comfortable with. Personality states sounds, well, too personal. Some play nice, but some would kill you with your own nose for crossing them and then laugh. Don't say this out loud, but I don't want some of them to be me. I don't want to hurt their feelings, but they're fucking exhausting.

Perhaps I've lost my mind, but I can see it. A dim glowing, tucked away in a corner. Somewhere I knew it would be safe, where I knew I could find it again. But I can't see which freaking corner. I think if I lost my keys, I'd find my mind lying right next to them. I can't afford to lose my keys to test the theory, but what kind of hassle is it to lose your mind?

But in the end, I am the one who ignores the whispers; the ghosts of memories best left forgotten. The whispers hammer my head, pounding my soul into recognition of what I left behind, all in memoriam to tales yet to tell. I subdue the pounding back into the secrets, the ghosts I love more than any other, the stories built to fit what I need to feel, what I need to be. Learning to be like him.

TC Boyd

Sander Roscoe Wolff — *Ensconced*

"Sometimes the people who most need to reach out are the people least capable of it." — Jane Espenson

Amanda Matheus

Robin Axworthy

Stained

He sits on the couch, his head in hands.
Daddy what's wrong? she asks.
His brother has just died, hit by a truck on the highway—
walked out in front of it some say,
or was unseen. No one knows.

His grandfather drank cyanide one night.
No one knows why.
His wife found him in the barn next morning.
His business was good,
his wife and children loved him.

It scares her to see him cry like a child,
like she does when she is sad and afraid,
gulping down the air as if it could balloon
away the horror, the untenable knowing.

He was already taking uppers by then,
though she won't know until much later.
He drove through the dark at night
to barns warm with cow breath and manure
to treat milk fevers; then was up
before breakfast to start surgery
and more calls. He loved her and the rest
but didn't know how to make it
under the circumstances. He drank beer
with lunch, whiskey after dinner. At night
he swallowed downers, but who knew?

Later, she spins away, into paisley, headbands,
fringed boots, cheap wine, weed, a little acid.
She cannot understand any of it. She swims
into her life, flailing desperately to keep
from drowning. Her sisters spin too,
twisting on the lines of their love,
on the lies that suckled them from birth,
hooks sunk deep into their guts. They don't know
how to cut themselves loose. Jobs, love, children –
still the wine can't numb the darkness shadowing them,
the way they all look over their shoulders,
check the stove over and over to make sure it's out,
unplug lights in case, of fire, start awake at night,
hearts racing, as if the nightmare were still under the bed.

It helps in later years, when the stories bubble forth and coalesce:
the full moon night their grandfather planted the front yard
with corn, the way he used to chase their father through the desert,
screaming murder but sobbing into his hands instead, collapsed;
the way when the oldest brother died at thirteen, their father's heart
was torn open with no one to stitch it back together except himself,

and they count themselves lucky he did not walk
out into the road
or drink poison
or take a final ride on the needles in his veins.

Now, she watches her daughter carefully,
fearing arthritis and heart disease on her husband's side,
but fearing even more the black despair that runs
in her veins, this stone at her core, a weight
against dance; not knowing if she, too,
inherited this hollow opening, this stain
that leaches light into dark.

Painted Storm — Yeggi Kaela Watts

Jane Roe

Static, seeking memory

With a bit of friction, ions run, opposites, away from each other.
Then the negatives want to jump back on the positives.

I had a dream last night
that I was three when the incest began.
I have wanted to know.
I have had ways of counting.
The earliest memories, what room where they in?
Which sisters had left home?
The one I had seen with him,
looking passive, or was it paralyzed?
It matters, because they say you get weird when your child
reaches the age you were
when it happened.
My children approach the age
that is all I know.

One year for Christmas I got a vanity,
a plastic desk with screw-in plastic legs,
a pull-up mirror and a chair just my size.
Most of my incest memories are of fear
or despair, but this one I thought the earliest
is of anger and annoyance.
I guess I was still self-possessed at the time.
It's so hard to remember such a state.
I must have had no words,
      no concepts, no context
other than God and the devil, and why
would he choose me to drag to hell with him?
And my own first vanity,
      which I thought was great
      (and he was interrupting my play).

He came up from behind and asked
if he could help brush my hair.
Attention! (still a good thing) A glorious present,
affirming my beauty, and attention to boot!
Sure! But with one hand he held his dick
and looked at it in the mirror,
my hair and shoulder just a frame
within the frame.
              Static.
"You need two hands to brush hair,"
I said with annoyance and disgust.
One to brush, one to hold down the hair
that tries to fly away.

I've always remembered the vanity incident
but not thought it mattered,
so it is not as layered as other memories
      the memories slathered
      with memories of remembering
      of meaning, of telling,
      of interpretation, analysis, distance.
Today, though, this memory seems
      to be the exact moment I learned:
      To be attractive is dangerous.

My mind was so simple then.
 To remember further back is like imagining
the mind of a cat,
or Alzheimer's, or being somebody else.

I fear the vivid, the raw, the unlayered memory:
as if I would re-experience it all
without my current mind's defenses,
without understanding,
suspended.

Another layer:
If that was the first violation, why annoyance?
Annoyance seems to say, "Oh, you again.
Get away, pest!"

              Static.

In the mirror, I cannot see my face.

Sarah A. Davis
True Colors

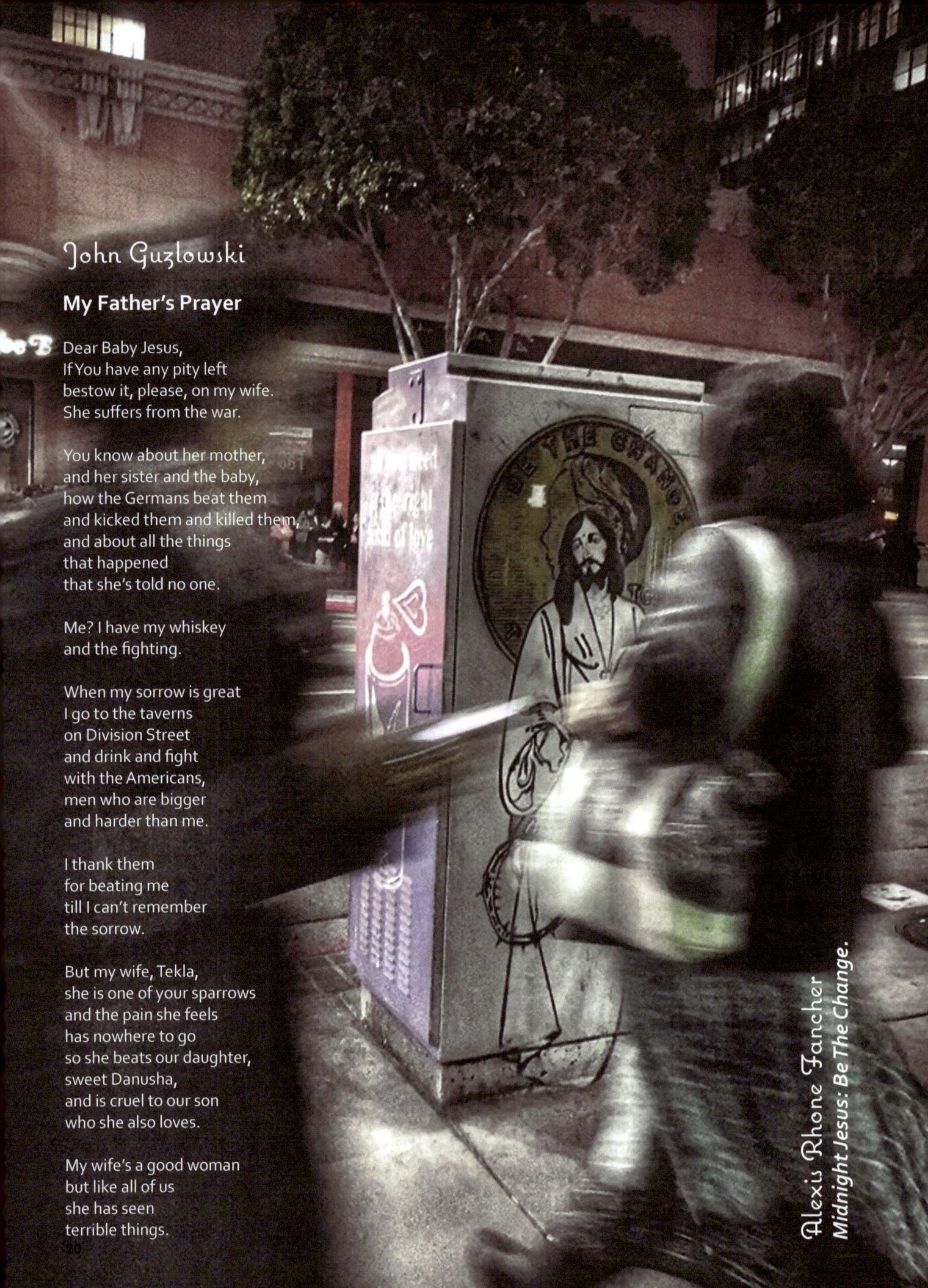

John Guzlowski

My Father's Prayer

Dear Baby Jesus,
If You have any pity left
bestow it, please, on my wife.
She suffers from the war.

You know about her mother,
and her sister and the baby,
how the Germans beat them
and kicked them and killed them,
and about all the things
that happened
that she's told no one.

Me? I have my whiskey
and the fighting.

When my sorrow is great
I go to the taverns
on Division Street
and drink and fight
with the Americans,
men who are bigger
and harder than me.

I thank them
for beating me
till I can't remember
the sorrow.

But my wife, Tekla,
she is one of your sparrows
and the pain she feels
has nowhere to go
so she beats our daughter,
sweet Danusha,
and is cruel to our son
who she also loves.

My wife's a good woman
but like all of us
she has seen
terrible things.

Alexis Rhone Fancher
Midnight Jesus: Be The Change.

Natalie Hirt

A Birthday Visit to My Brother

He lies on the floor rocking in a human pretzel shape, crying partly out loud in a wail and partly silent with his head tilted back. For a moment, in some grotesque way, he reminds me of our dog lying out on the back porch snapping at flies.

I step into the room, barely. I'm afraid to go further to smell the stink. What is it? Urine? Yes, it's that, but also too many medications, rotting in a secret corner of the walls and carpet.

His adult diaper is bunched on one side and I can see through the skeletal angles of his body; he's nearly sexless. I only know he's a man because I knew him as a baby boy, bright and hopeful, when Sesame Street books could light up his eyes and make the dimples play on his face. When I taught him how to rainbow-write his name.

He will die long before his time. He knows it, too. Maybe that's why he's crying in the fly-snapping pretzel shape. He's nipping it back and back, the death, the illness, the insanity. Get away!

I step in closer, allow myself to be a part.

"Why are you crying, Johnny?" I ask him softly.

He stops howling, turning his face away from the wall to look at me. Something registers in his eyes. He recognizes me and straightens his legs a bit. Still staring, he lies there, quieted, snapping.

The second hand of the clock above moves forward against each snap of his jaw. Click-tick, click-tick. If only I could lift him out of himself.

"Nnatalie. It's yoour birthday. Nnatalie." And he smiles, his face a wall of teeth because there's hardly any skin.

I ache, wanting to reach out, to touch him, and hug his bare arms full of self-inflicted scratches. But I can't. I'm afraid of his voices, but more that, I'm repulsed. I don't want to get too close to the red, puffy gums or the drool on the side of his face. I don't want his disease to touch me.

"Yes, Johnny, it's my birthday," I say. I can't help smiling. How does he know these things?

I look around the room while he slowly draws out each word, "What wasz yoour fay-vo-rite yeeear?"

"I don't have a favorite age," I say. And I'm not going to cry even though I already know what's coming.

"Miine is foourteen," he says, gnashing his teeth together.

I know that year. It was the last year he'd go to school. The last year I'd see him in those eyes, wearing that skin, before he was officially institutionalized.

When I leave, I'm numb.

He remembered my birthday.

Driving home, I see that people are eating. Walking, too. Sunlight filters through trees. Back there, behind me, my little brother uncurled and smiled even though I left him. Even though I went on home to celebrate another healthy year.

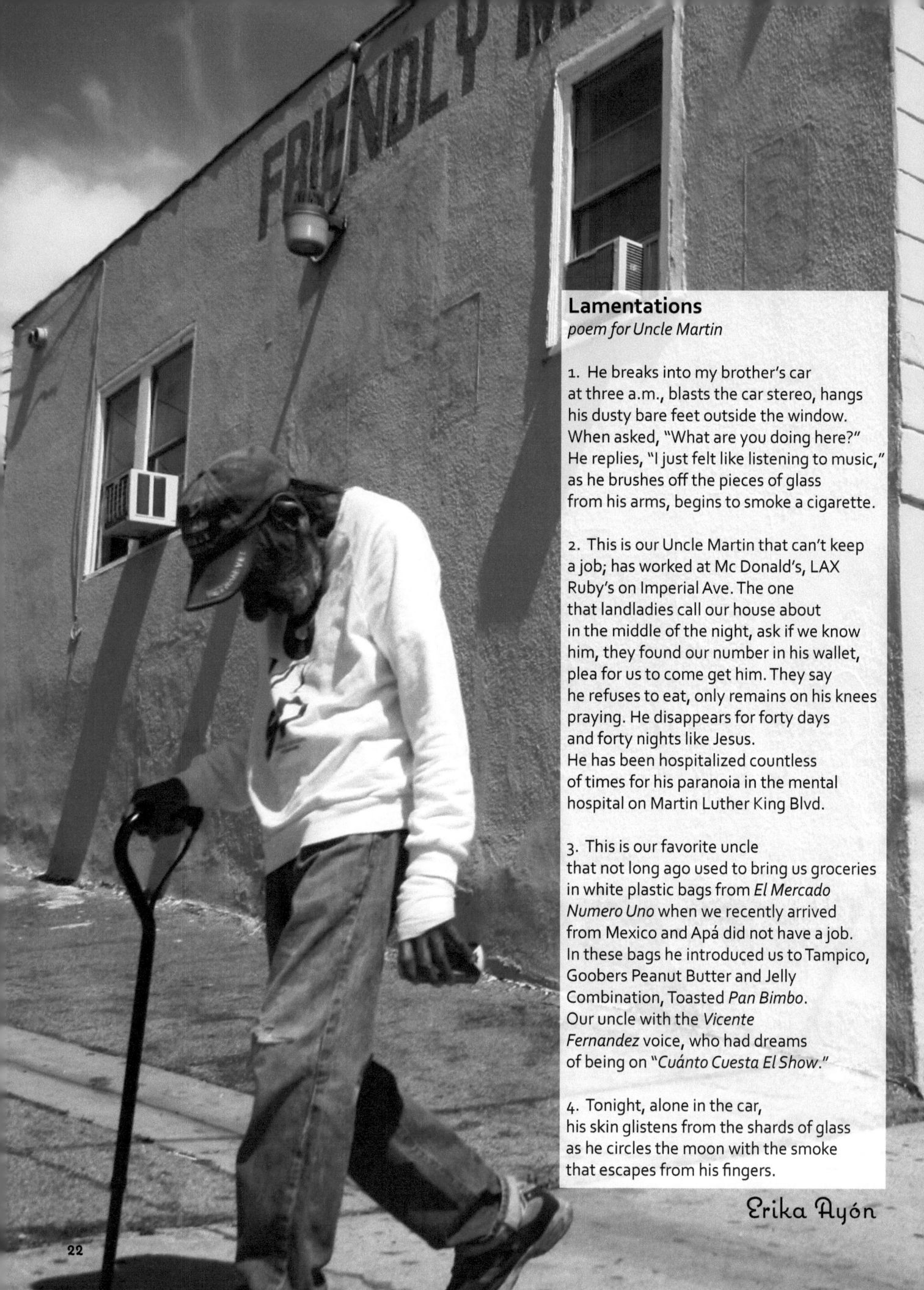

Lamentations
poem for Uncle Martin

1. He breaks into my brother's car
at three a.m., blasts the car stereo, hangs
his dusty bare feet outside the window.
When asked, "What are you doing here?"
He replies, "I just felt like listening to music,"
as he brushes off the pieces of glass
from his arms, begins to smoke a cigarette.

2. This is our Uncle Martin that can't keep
a job; has worked at Mc Donald's, LAX
Ruby's on Imperial Ave. The one
that landladies call our house about
in the middle of the night, ask if we know
him, they found our number in his wallet,
plea for us to come get him. They say
he refuses to eat, only remains on his knees
praying. He disappears for forty days
and forty nights like Jesus.
He has been hospitalized countless
of times for his paranoia in the mental
hospital on Martin Luther King Blvd.

3. This is our favorite uncle
that not long ago used to bring us groceries
in white plastic bags from *El Mercado
Numero Uno* when we recently arrived
from Mexico and Apá did not have a job.
In these bags he introduced us to Tampico,
Goobers Peanut Butter and Jelly
Combination, Toasted *Pan Bimbo*.
Our uncle with the *Vicente
Fernandez* voice, who had dreams
of being on "*Cuánto Cuesta El Show*."

4. Tonight, alone in the car,
his skin glistens from the shards of glass
as he circles the moon with the smoke
that escapes from his fingers.

Erika Ayón

Liquor Store Junkie Boris Ingles

Namesake

Aunt Kathy was my namesake. She came to our house that summer day to visit with my mother, offer warmhearted my-how-you've-growns to nieces, nephews. Her two little boys ran outside to join my younger siblings on our giant tree swing. I watched them from the window, three aboard as one walked the swing in circles, the ropes twisting tighter and higher. When the ropes doubled up and not one more step could be taken, the swing was released, a tornado of ropes unfurling with a speed that sent their legs flying, their heads yanked back with screams. "Let's make Kathy tea." Mother led me to the kitchen.

Aunt Kathy was named after St. Catherine. This didn't make sense until I learned Kathleen is the Irish form of Catherine. While baby name books merely mention courage and purity, the Irish know her story. A famine hit and people crawled across the countryside for food. The Devil himself appeared and promised he'd feed them all to their fill if they'd only give up their souls to him. Countess Cathleen offered her own pure soul instead, saving the people from starvation and an eternity of flames. At the moment of her final breath, the Devil returned to collect her soul when God stopped him, declaring her sacrifice so selfless it could not end with such an injustice.

Downstairs in our family room, Kathy waited for us. I knew she was alone but I could hear her speaking, soft, fluttering words like butterflies being released up the stairs. I chose a pretty teacup for her. The flowers reminded me of the wild garden knotted round her house. When steam shrieked from the kettle, Kathy yelled out "Uh-oh!" until we stopped the whistle.

Mother looked me in the eye, spoke in a low, steady tone about a call from my aunt's husband, how Kathy flushed her medications, smashed their television with a baseball bat, wept over the world's wickedness. "Don't be afraid." Mother patted my shoulder. As we descended the stairs, Kathy quieted, her smile as familiar as our visits to her house where canned foods from her charities filled her own family room beyond any other use. "The poor are family, too," she would say.

Kathy tried to drink her tea, to discuss planning an anniversary party for my grandparents, but her hand trembled and her voice rose in pitch as if she found herself ten years old again. She screamed, "Mama left me alone with the baby. And I didn't see her crawl away to the neighbor's. Their driveway was brick. Red, jagged bricks. Her little face, oh her face!" Mother rushed from the house. "My little sister's scars," Kathy cried. "Did you know they sent me to a convent?" I tried to comfort her, to stand down the Devil for Kathy, but in my heart, I swore at a god who abandons his saints to a life of torment before blessing them on a cold deathbed.

Nina Johnson

In My Robe

They let me walk alone—
barefoot
in the grass, where AM gardens
are wilted with afternoon
thoughts
the only statues on these grounds
are memories frozen inside my head.
Blurred with prescription haze
to cloud my mind towards
forgetfulness
my little colored friends help me
from succumbing to the familiar
aftertaste of pain; I would love to feel
something…
dirt, rocks, anything
under my blistered feet. Reeling
like I'm stuck inside this record
broken—
surreally struck, I am
inside this same loop; dizzy
confused
to be caught within this
maze like I'm reliving scenes
from my own shining without
shades too bright for my red eyes;
blinking
which way to focus
my worried footsteps. Trying
to remember how I get back
to my solitary room.

Looking
for any pockets of answers,
a handful of dead air behind
my lifeless grips; I feel
nothing
underneath this white robe,
these white masked orderlies
who took my belt to keep me
from feeling all the inner
breaking
of my softest shell. I refuse to realize
or follow the flows of regurgitating
madness
choking through my missing
necklace—gold stained gagging
to keep myself from laughing,
crying
or anything without meaning
but swallowing to forget where
I misplaced my next pill, I keep
awakening
to lost voices
diagnosing the constant changes
of moods, my mouth is strapped
I feel choked, no words come out,
like confusion trapped
inside
this aching throat.

Adrian Cepeda

Jackie Joice *Remnants*

Her Suitcase

They packed a suitcase with more clothes,
to take it to the hospital. She could
wear clothes, street clothes, in the hospital.
No gown needed to probe the interior.
There were clothes she wanted
to wear, and they could be packed up and taken
to her. Stay with her, no bother.
She needed more clothes. The ones she had
were not enough. With the time passing, she needed
more clothes.
Pairs of pants, some blouses, a bathrobe.
These were necessities.
I watched them come together, like a daughter.
The suitcase was a need that
could not be denied. She needed more clothes
for the weeks to follow. Street clothes were allowed in.
She wanted these clothes, certain
ones but not others. These clothes were desires
and they could be understood, collected, and brought
to her. She is not at the bus stop
without any clothes on. She wants them now.
The clothes are weeks. The clothes are
weeks apart from me.

Nina Bannett

Tobi Alfier

The Artist

Sometimes she does not feel like telling a story
words just so, no room for misunderstanding
misdirection miscommunication misogyny
misspelling no one to blame, no one to blame her
no victim no pain no desire yes desire no platitudes
no triteness no line breaks no punctuation sometimes
the page cannot contain the words the smells the tears
the inadequacy the rage the vision the magnitude
the inescapable adverbs sometimes,
there are no adverbs.

Sometimes she sees herself with arms outstretched
braced against the currents that purport to drown
she will not allow it she takes the letters the damning
words the hateful words the heretic words the lies
the lies the lies the lies she cuts them into little pieces
delusional
              sabotage
                          indefensible
                                      insane
                                              I hate you
I love you she buries them deep within canvases
and collages an artist imprinting her work with DNA
she buries them deep under colors and columns, pieces
of cork Starbucks coffee containers cherubs and trees
she buries them under seas and skies the letters turning
golden and poisoning someone else's house, not hers.

Sometimes she just has to get off the fucking bus
be angry scream at the top of a mountain not ask
for help hurtle the minutiae from more than one surface
not sweep it up leave it there until it rots
paint the French dictionary 8 feet by 10 cut her hair
and burn
the wedding album.
The calm is a blessing
now she can get back to words.

Kerfe Roig *Lunatic*

Amanda Mathews

"The waves are breaking, the wind is singing and it just won't stop."

Daniel McGinn

The Dark

1.
My family, in a tight circle gazed across the bonfire.

My mother's hair was full of sparks, her eyes were raw as onions

and the sky started falling
out of both sides of her mouth.

When she spoke to me
her voice scraped my back,

the hills behind her blossomed into flames,

my impaled marshmallow began to turn,

from soft skin to scab, from stiff skin to pus,

I was one of the children,
all of our coat hangers were glowing.

2.
Twenty years have passed. I am half asleep

on my bed, a gun
sticking out of my mouth.

She asks, Are you dreaming?
She asks, How have you been sleeping?

Off and on, I think,
all things come and go.

A fire burns in my chest. I've been feeding it,

it takes something away every time I breathe.

I slide down deeper underneath the blanket.
Where are you going?

My mother's disembodied voice asks,
Where have you been?

Then the wind approaches like a whore,

no one summons it but the fire loves it.

Half-awake now, my mind drifts with a car, into opposing traffic,

the bed jerks and I startle her. This is real.

I keep hurting myself. Now the fire has spread

to the hills behind the highway, the waves are breaking,

the wind is singing and it just won't stop.

Sitting in a Burning House

Donald Illich

The chair shoots up in flame.
Cereal boxes on top of the fridge
instantly vaporize when they're touched
by fire. The sofa is a black mark
on the floor. Front windows leave
melted glass on the sidewalk.
You sit, eating your microwaved
meal. Pasta smokes in your mouth.
You don't see that anything is burning.
The chair is solid, not disintegrating
as you touch it. Your fork is not pouring
hot metal into your mouth. But you do
notice how the clock keeps moving.
And that you better go to sleep soon,
or you will have trouble getting up.
Your parents may be gone in the next
few years. You could leave with them,
in that void that swallows up everything.
As you stand up, you don't realize
that your hair is singed, your eyes
are exploding, your mouth burnt.
You have enjoyed your meal.
You brush your teeth with fire.
You sleep in a bed full of flames.

Boris Ingles

Iridescence of Night

On Your Birthday, Mamá

Mark Smith-Soto

Eavesdropping on the silence
where you once were resonant,
I have trouble hearing you laugh—

strange because memory says
how funny you could be, knew
how to squeeze a joke until its
ribs cracked.
         I see you clearly,
head thrown back, arms
in the air, giving yourself up.
totally tickled.
            But I can't hear you.

For your birthday,
as a gift to me more than to you,
I wanted to bring your laughter

into this poem, have it take its place
among mattering things. I haven't
managed it, Tulita, but I'll keep

trying, because too long I've been
the shepherd of your tears, gathering
and holding them so close to me

I could no longer tell them from my own.

Michele Rene *Mourning*

The Museum

It's funny how you can only see
a relationship clearly after it's over.
After the last time your mouths part,
the first time you know they won't meet again.
After the fight over who makes the plans more often.
After you borrow his shirt
without any intention of giving it back,
and after the ink from his notes in your books
settles into the pages in permanence.

The last time you sleep in his bed,
you won't know it's the last time.
Only after the trinkets of memories are
spilled from your mind
do you start to remember.
In the museum of your past,
your artifacts become an exhibit
before your eyes.

Once the clutter is cleared,
you remember the time he told you
your shirt made him uncomfortable.
That he *didn't want other guys looking at you*.
You were his, after all, and *you don't know how that feels*.
And the times you agreed to get him off
even though you weren't in the mood anymore
because you felt guilty for wanting to stop.
The mess might have been too comforting.

The three times you tried to break up with him,
your own words coming out of your mouth
sounded like a foreign language,
felt like sharp sea glass on your tongue.
He kissed your mouth, dry with ocean salt,
licked it clean of all resistance.

He reminded you that two people
with a gallery of love like yours
could never be wrong for each other.
You didn't say anything about how
everything he looked at had already happened.
That right now, you felt trapped by his room,
his body, the air around both of you.
You poured your words into his lungs,
the ones you rehearsed that never made it into the air.

Sometimes you still think he didn't know what he was doing.
Or maybe you hope that, to keep yourself sane.
Once, over cigarettes, he told your best friend
he was good at manipulating people.
He meant manipulating people
into giving him cigarettes. You think.

You still wonder how
you wilted over time.
How someone who held your jaw
so gently crushed your words
to powder before your eyes,
and you stayed.
You will not have a name for this.
You thought without bruises or swearing
there was nothing wrong.

As you clear out the relics in your museum,
you wonder how you didn't see it.
Because there was no tragedy, no big event,
it was a slow build.
A collection.
A curating of moments
that only meant something
in reflection. In thoughtful observation,
head tilted to the side, a pensive sigh,

It's funny how he did that–
not how I let it happen,
it's funny, what he did.
Because it taught you
to choose your treasures wisely,
to dissect each artifact
under a microscope and know
that you deserve only the most precious ones.

Anna Szilagyi

Leah Mueller

Texas Midlife Crisis
        (A letter to my sister)

Dear Ericka,

Exactly three months have passed since you sat in your small American car, faced a red and white-striped barrier sign on a dead-end road outside of Houston, shoved a gun barrel underneath your breast, pulled the trigger, and died without bleeding. Your aim was so good that even in death, you knew how to lodge the barrel in the spot where your bones would collapse like a planned demolition, and there would be no spray to clean up later. I still don't know how you managed that.

For the first week, your husband refused to look in your car for the bullet, and thought it was still lodged in your body, which was already scheduled for cremation. After the funeral, I asked to see your car, because it was the last thing you had touched before you texted "goodbye" and pulled the trigger. He had parked it casually in the garage, after he pulled his Datsun 240Z out into the driveway, and washed his car's exterior clean of debris. Its body shimmered in the driveway now, like a polished silver gun barrel. He always did love that Datsun, and was glad to have an excuse to drive it again.

The two of us opened the door of your vehicle, and peered inside at the cushioned seat where you deliberately took your last breaths, noted its puzzling lack of any human remnants. For a moment, he seemed almost like you might imagine a grieving husband to be—his breath shortened, and he ran his hand across the underside of the driver's seat, and finally said, "I found a hole." With one forefinger, he traced the bullet hole, like you might examine a tiny wound that had inexplicably failed to heal. He ran his other hand under the seat, but came up empty. He shook his head, and said, "The police must have taken the bullet."

Later, we drove a mile from the house to the place where you died, and your husband kept getting lost. He complained that GPS had failed to store the data, but that it was more fitting for us to drive aimlessly, as you had probably done. I doubt if you drove aimlessly— you had probably scoped out the spot months in advance. You had already compiled a funeral music set list, checked your life insurance policy, and sent farewell flowers that were scheduled to arrive at your house after your husband discovered your body. It wasn't necessary, because all of his friends sent flowers—they arrived continuously for a week until they covered every surface in the house.

Your husband took three towering racks of sympathy bouquets, placed them strategically in a row beside the sign that marked the place where you had died, then took a rapid-fire series of photos with his phone. I wondered why he couldn't seem to stop texting everywhere he went, even when he was driving, until he was finally at your funeral, and had to place his folded hands in his lap.

As soon as the memorial was over, we dined at your house on baked beans and white bread, and everyone dove right in, except for one of your co-workers, who stood at the side of the group, refusing to eat. Your husband mingled, phone in hand, pressing the tiny buttons with earnest concentration, while your adult children cried in the corner with their father. I argued politics with Texas Republicans and counted the hours before I could go home, because everyone had forgotten how to grieve in the middle of so many electronic diversions, and I'd forgotten how much I hated Texas.

You were nowhere in attendance, even though your photos spun in circles on the television screen—you with your husband, standing on your lawn in front of the "sold" sign, you and your daughter before you quit speaking to each other, even a couple of photos of the two of us that I had deliberately forgotten. We hadn't seen each other for ten years, and I'd never met your children, not even once, because their father took them to Mexico after the divorce. You were goddamn well not going to subject yourself to the crass indignity of another divorce, you much preferred to die instead.

The joke is on you, however, because your husband never found the bullet, and doesn't know what to do with your ashes, so he keeps them on a shelf in his closet. He announced on Facebook a month later that he was in Love, then posted photographs of himself, grinning hugely as he stood with his arm around a prettier woman, and I finally realized why he did so much texting after you died.

If I was a gun-toting Texas Republican, I would suggest that your aim was cockeyed, and you shot the wrong person, but I've never held a firearm, let alone pulled a trigger, and I don't recommend it to anybody. I wish you had spared yourself, however, and sued your worthless husband for everything, left him penniless and bleeding in the dust.

I always thought you were the survivor, hiding behind the cactus with a pistol, that you would bravely fight your adversaries until, exhausted, they finally surrendered, and that I was the one who would either make a mess, or miss the target entirely. Yet I am alive, on a drab October evening, at the beginning of the Northwest rainy season, staring at my own winter from the other side of the barrel, and I have no plans to leave here any time soon.

I understand why you can't answer this letter, and hope your death is like the vacation you kept denying yourself when you were alive. Your daughter took a photo of herself in her underwear, and posted it as her profile picture on Facebook, so life does continue, and you really can't blame it for that. If you have the chance, wink at me from the clouds, and in your next life, please stay the hell away from Jeremiah and Texas.

Love,

Your sister, Leah

Nancy Correro

What it's like Now
for my brother, Michael

I've decided to wear your ring
on a chain
around my neck—
with its colorful stones
embedded in gold.

It makes me think of the pills you took—
all the colors of the rainbow.
I keep wanting to gather all your things,
and replace them in your house
just as we found them—
chocolates in the freezer,
clothes in the dryer,
dog on her bed
wondering
when you'd wake.

I keep waiting for you to appear and tell me
to take the ring off—anything to piss you off again.
All the girls from high school are still talking about you
on Facebook—how you were their first crush.

I want to unwind it all,
and rearrange your last days,
and repair the circle
you thought was incomplete.

For now, I'll flip through your albums and CDs,
and read your old letters and piece together
last words spoken,
and wear this gaudy rainbow ring.

Jackie Joice
Suppressed

Andrew Brown

Tidying Up After Helen

I have changed the sheets on which we did lie, on my now cold king size bed where once, what seems eons ago, I watched you sleep, your naked body wondrous to my eye.
I have washed the bath towel I laughingly, softly, dried, caressed and tickled you with.
I have reluctantly, reticently, placed mementoes of you in a separate special box.
I have placed all your e-mails into a supposedly never-to-be-opened folder.
I have finally stopped smelling your pillow's aroma.
I have stopped placing your towel against my nose and softly inhaling, reminiscing.
I have taken the screen saver picture of you from my desktop, you remember, you know the one, with the cormorants in the foreground and the Docks and the M Shed in the background and you with those gorgeous, deep pool eyes and laughing smile complementing the view!
I have taken your jars of food and your special dietary health supplements from the fridge and the cupboards.
I have moved the well-played CD's and DVD's to out-of-sight places.
I have vacuumed the lounge floor where we danced and made love.
Stubborn strands of your greying long hair remain embedded in my blood red carpet.

Victoria Griffin

Rung My Bell

    Hard play. Quick blow to the helmet. Knock against the dirt.
    Get up. Run the bases. "I'm fine. Just rung my bell."
    Ignore it, I'm not dizzy. Play the ball, the middle one. Leave without asking for help. Painkiller. I'm fine.
    Sleep, wake. Can't speak. Door closes like a gunshot. Turn the light on, the world goes white. The sound of my own voice is a mallet to my eardrums.
    The world hurts. They send me out anyway. Ask me to step through halls, people swarming, everything attacking me. Take a pill, you won't feel it. I fall and don't know if it hurts.
    Want to read, try to see the words as letters, meaning. Can't. Just see white and black, white and black, gray. Everything is gray. Everything is blurred. I want to understand. I try to understand. I watch and listen and hear and smell and see and everything is flying in on me at once like birds pecking out my eyes and dousing me in bleach. It burns it burns it burns—
    Corner. Dark. Close my eyes. Rock back and forth, back and forth. My fingers draw closed. The nails make red marks in my palms. My arms are pinned tight to my stomach, and my knees press against my forehead. I forget to breathe. My neck arches forward, protecting my face, straining, pain. My whole body tightens into a ball, muscles clamped against bones.
    I rock back and forth, back and forth.
    "I'm fine," I told them. "I'm fine. Just rung my bell."

Michael Cantin

Second Sunday, May 1997

I am very nearly a man and this is the first time
my Stepfather and I have ever played catch.
Our tosses are listless as first,
heavy with the leaden weight of uncertainty.
It is so quiet that the air itself can be heard
slapping angrily against the pigskin,
begging us to stop the fucking wake already.

Our arms instead become catapults
while our lips remain still:
the sealed bank vaults of our faces.
Not that we had all that much to say before.
Nothing to say before the fire,
or before the medications,
or before the bad dreams.
Before the long goodbyes met by drooling half kisses
or the promises more empty than her gaze.

The football does the speaking for us now:
ts path waivers into an assault.
Its arc stretches into an unanswered question.
It is bullet that smashes into the pulverized meat
of my chest again and again
and again.

Starry Eyed

Ricardo Vidana

Convenience Store

I went to the convenience store,
he says. He is a family friend.
I pick him up in front of his
apartment building.
It's Thanksgiving or Passover.
I only see him twice a year.
He doesn't have a car.
I pick him up,
he sits in the passenger seat.
He complains about his knees—arthritis,
complains about not finding a job
at his age.

He smells like soap today.
I told him he couldn't come into the car
if he didn't shower.
His nails are long, ridged,
some of them split, broken,
peeling off.
Maybe some kind of mineral
deficiency, some medication's side effect.
Must be uncomfortable
to maneuver in life
with your nails getting caught everywhere—
socks, sleeves, sweaters.
I don't think he cares.

He is clean shaven,
has missed some stubble
on the left chin—
there is always something.
It looks like an island
of dead grass.

I went to the convenience store,
he says,
*and I bought a soda
and a candy bar.
But I didn't have
enough money.
I needed 25 cents more.
The girl in the store
took out 25 cents
from her own pocket.
The next day I went back
and I put the 25 cents
in the penny jar.
I think she was happy to see me.*

How old is she? I ask.

*Probably my age,
but she looks younger*, he says.

*She opened a can of soda,
when I went back,
you know,
and we passed it back and forth.
I told her that she was pretty.
We have the same taste in music,
and I started talking
about the bands I know,
because I was in a band.
I played electric guitar.
We went everywhere, in a bus.
I made a list.*

You made a list. I say.

*A list of all the things
I want to tell her.
I don't want to forget.
It has happened to me before,
that I forget.
I have to practice.
Can I practice with you?
Like, I think of you all the time,
and you were so kind
when you put the 25 cents
from your pocket
and I was in a band
before
and we should go out
to a concert or something,
and I want to touch you.*

He covers his mouth
with his hands,
like a child.

Mariano Zaro

Ednos

Growing up with three younger brothers and two struggling parents, I didn't always get a full plate to eat. Only sometimes was I resentful of that. Growing up all legs and third tallest in elementary class—thin limbs, knocking knees, and slightly protruding belly—my mom would say I looked like one of those starving African children, an image of daytime charity commercials. The entirety of how fucked up that was, was missed on me for years. Growing up with bookshelves of diet and clean eating books, cleanses were just another thing adults did. Dinners were things moms didn't always have.

In 5th grade, a classmate of mine fainted on her way to lunch. Opening up her Disney princess bag, the teacher found it empty and scolded her before the rest of us. I'm not sure the nurse or her parents were ever told.

In 6th grade, one of my favorite shows was America's Next Top Model. I remember standing before mirrors until I couldn't, aware that I didn't look like those beautiful people, my body awkward and too much. Always too much. I remember knowing I would never be the runway model this little boy once dreamed of. My mother said I "filled out." At that time, I had never hated two words more.

In 9th grade, I always wore ill-fitting clothes to hide myself. Ashamed of all the places skin didn't pull tight across bone. The only purpose they served was for the serrated bread knife that my mother still can't find.

In 12th grade, I learned what the face of an "advanced-stage" eating disorder looked like. Scarecrows of people that frightened me like a bird. I became obsessed with numbers despite never being all that good at math. Scrubbed bathrooms clean more times than my mother ever wrote on my chore list. Learned what a sick sense of pride really meant whenever I was told I looked unwell. Bought an expensive pair of pants I only barely fit into once... that I still keep in the back of my closet.

It's the only part of me I've ever insisted was "just a phase." A phase that's denied me of more than I ever denied myself. A phase I don't imagine myself ever growing out of (I'm so scared of growing). All I've ever wanted was to be as small as I've always been made to feel. As noncommittal as my disorder. Eating disorder, not otherwise specified. Ednos.

Taylor Flynn

Michele Rene *Posture*

Ellen Stone

Bees in the wall

It's no wonder I am always full
what with the way the mind goes on
like bees + bees + hives hunkering
inside the porch wall, really attached there
like putty + stucco + all the soft things
that harden in the dark, from the beginning
as in soft/move/forward to stuck/glued/burgeoning
but in a sad way like you can't get out of.
I suspect I could pour a drink tonight,
whiskey or rye, scotch, something I don't
even like the taste of & I could sit it on the bare
counter + add ice cubes + drink the glass full
in the empty afternoon, like my dad used to.
And, then I could do it again & before you know it,
I would be stuck—like he was, or is. But maybe then,
I could understand it. Like leaving bees in the walls
for years, because you love them, the way the honey
smell permeated the living room when maybe that
was the only sweetness you could count on. Why
bees might be the best roommates, actually. So social,
but solitary, all the same. Their company, the easy glide
of bee, how they hang in air, or go exactly where they
need to, no lingering apology, or diverging purposes.

Sarah Lim *Rising*

Cleopatre in Pont Avinon — Stephen Linsteadt

Asperguilty

My crime is
Life by Misadventure;
no Penal Code number, but quite
politically incorrect, a reckless,
raging dance on thin ice.
I really am sorry for those
Wagnerian meltdowns and
Shakespearian night terrors,
the mistempered child now grown
into a woman who writes poetry while
driving in the rain, for fuck's sake.
I'm sorry for the warped
vinyl of my children,
scratchy, hauntingly
beautiful, pocked
by my outbursts, and
summoned too often to answer
for my sins.
I'm sorry that there
is, sometimes, too much beauty
for one skin to hold
and needs, sometimes,
venting, with
knives and razors.
Don't decode my chaos,
dangle diagnoses you
culled from dusty tomes;
I'm neither God's microchipped pet, nor
the devil's latest done girl.
Let my madness determine its own
method, let me walk in beauty, live
in screeching colors and disconcerting truths.
Let me spin, sing, flap my hands,
fire my furiants into the windshield.
Love me, laugh at my jokes, my ignoble
gasses, learn my triggers and
love the gun,
and when I blow,
run.

Laura Saint Martin

Anxiety

looks like
            shrapnel
and fog
like sleep
            without the sleep

without the
                        jar
of   being
alive except
            survival
                        which looks like
not surviving

but shallow breath
            eyes that don't see
and

            petrification.

I am a stone

stuck forever
                        in the same
place   forever
holding my arms
                        aloft
beseeching
            change
      to come   and
save me

but
      change cannot
do anything
to stone   except
wear it down   more
            and more   until there
is
      nothing
            left but
dust.

K. Andrew Turner

Torrin Greathouse

Crooked Daisy
for Dash Teachout

Some nights I am afraid
I will outlive you, that a mother
I have never met, except in my nightmares
and your stories, will not send me
an invitation to your funeral.

That cigarette smoke will nest
in your lungs, like 1000 bees,
that cancer will honeycomb inside of you
till there is no room left to breathe.

Or that you will drown one night,
as though your mattress were a swimming pool,
as though vodka and Xanax were water wings,
as though that coffin were only
a submarine you would one day rise from.

Or that your synapses that sing
themselves into whispers and bending
violin strings unraveling will sing you
into dirt, into razorblade,
into woman made chandelier.

On those nights I wish
I could press your hand between mine
like a flower, keep it forever.

A crooked daisy,
never buried.
Never tasting dirt again.

Susan Solomon
Waiting for Spring

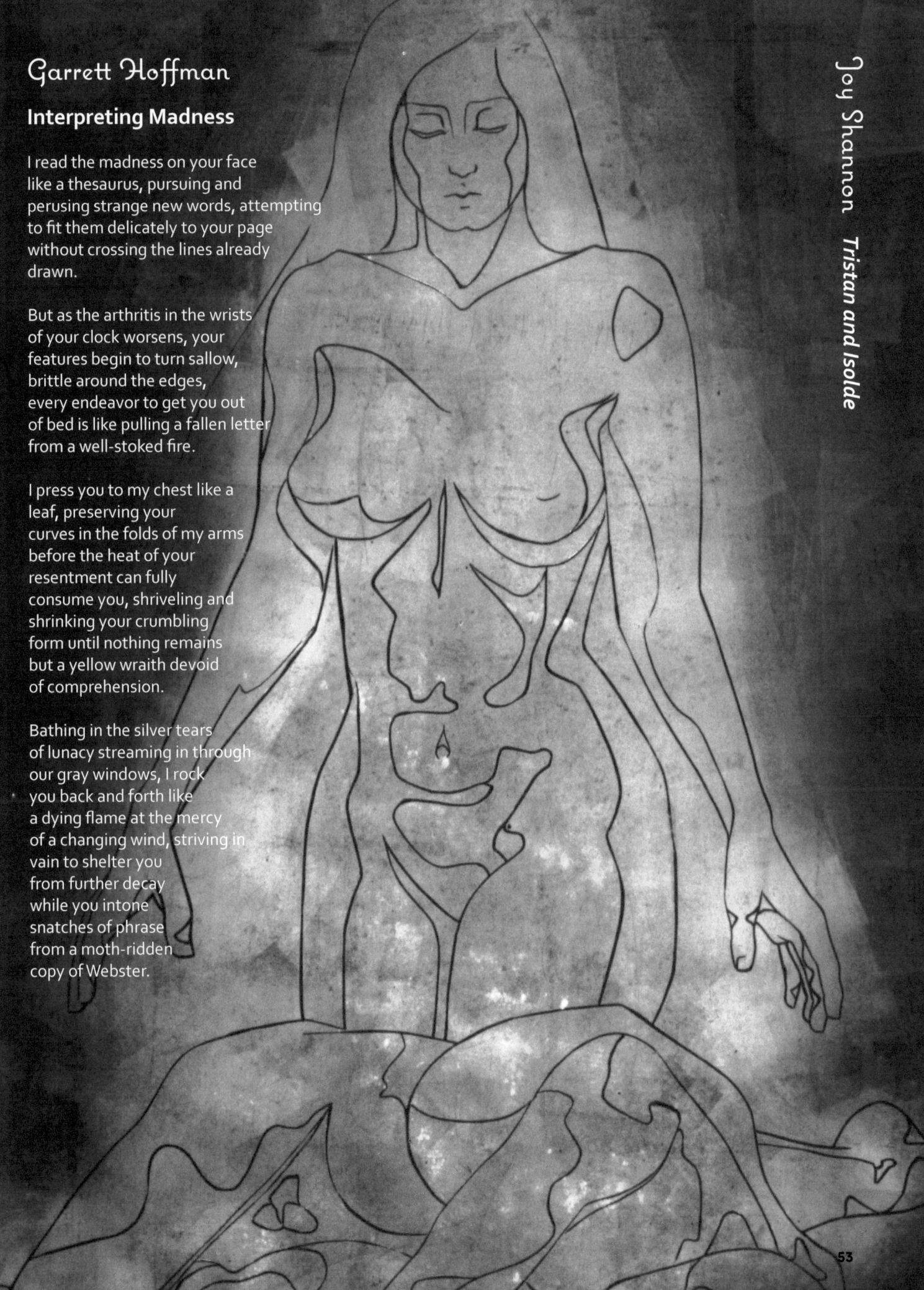

Garrett Hoffman

Interpreting Madness

I read the madness on your face
like a thesaurus, pursuing and
perusing strange new words, attempting
to fit them delicately to your page
without crossing the lines already
drawn.

But as the arthritis in the wrists
of your clock worsens, your
features begin to turn sallow,
brittle around the edges,
every endeavor to get you out
of bed is like pulling a fallen letter
from a well-stoked fire.

I press you to my chest like a
leaf, preserving your
curves in the folds of my arms
before the heat of your
resentment can fully
consume you, shriveling and
shrinking your crumbling
form until nothing remains
but a yellow wraith devoid
of comprehension.

Bathing in the silver tears
of lunacy streaming in through
our gray windows, I rock
you back and forth like
a dying flame at the mercy
of a changing wind, striving in
vain to shelter you
from further decay
while you intone
snatches of phrase
from a moth-ridden
copy of Webster.

Joy Shannon *Tristan and Isolde*

Laura Langston

Fasciculations

A lovely word that describes
the involuntary movements that can be secondary
to the death of neurons associated with ALS.
Sitting nervously in my car
waiting in your parking lot,
I hear your velvet voice echo in
the stairwell, followed by laughter.
Now I know you made it up the stairs,
an achievement unbearable to observe.
We don't hug—we will be touching so much,
the hug seems redundant.
We laugh in unison at nothing,
our voices so in pitch, it sounds musical.
Getting you into the Suburban,
the clinical part of my brain notes the
trembling with intention of your left leg
and the rigidity of that stubborn right foot.
I make a lame joke
and kiss your cheek as I buckle you safely upright.
Seeing your hand lying in your lap,
two fingers contracting into a claw;
I wonder how many times you have left
the pleasure of leaving your home
on your own two feet.
After the doctor visit you seem cheered;
we go to lunch and stuff our mouths,
grateful for the excuse to avoid conversation.
To let it all settle in.
I try not to sob into my sandwich.
Loving the sound of your machine gun laugh,
I try to keep you entertained with my stories,
because the sound of you laughing
makes me happy.
We cruise around the back roads,
admiring the woods and fields of farmed goodness.
You say with a sigh how much you love the journey
it's the only way you can get around now.
In my mind's eye,
I see you young and handsome,
leaping onto your stingray bicycle
and riding off to a new adventure,
brown as a Peruvian boy can be
on a hot shirtless summer.
I keep you out too long,
your head bobs in slumber
as I bounce over the potholes.
Upon arriving, after I help you
fall out of the car into the arms of your walker.

I make an excuse to go ahead
when I see you fumbling with your pants,
leaning against the dumpster.
Your eyes look frightened and ashamed
when you make it into the house,
asking me if I have ever peed on my shoes.
"Of course I have, I'm a girl!" I answer.
Neither of us laughs as you
wash your shoes in the sink.
You are tired now,
my heart is hurting and I don't want you
to comfort me.
I don't have any more jokes
so I kiss you goodbye as you settle into
your recliner
and cry my way back to the car.

Every Bird Its Nest A. Riding

Kristina England

Putting on a Face

When you stare at your hand long enough, it can become a desert, the smoothness of your youth baked into dry, rough sand. I never thought of age. I never thought of my hand before, but I am sick, and when people are sick, they observe the oddest of things. Beautiful, maybe, but when you don't have the answer to why your body is rupturing, you stare down your fist as if it would blow away in the next storm. *Don't go,* I think, but the pounds are shedding, the "thick-boned girl" is gone. I stare at my erosion, think to spread lotion on it, but cream is nothing more than a temporary fix. I look at my face in the mirror. It could be mounted on someone's wall, cheekbones pointing through skin. I put on makeup, my sandpaper fingers burrowing down into my face. I put on makeup though I can hardly swallow myself. Then I give my reflection one more dirty, betrayed look and leave for work, where everyone keeps looking at my wasteland, asking what the hell is going on. It is smiles (it has to be smiles) from here on out. "I'm fine. I'm fine," I'll say, as the sun beats hard and my body grows just a little more parched.

Joy Shannon *Death*

Metamorphoses and Mood Swings

Mary McCarthy

Sometimes I am Byzantine, winged
and intricate as an insect
with many jointed legs,
hard and jeweled as a beetle,
soft as a moth.
Sometimes I am sad, muddled
and formless, tired and full of rain.
My tears flow endlessly down,
a salty river,
where, like a new Ophelia,
I barely keep afloat,
and nothing can reach me.
Sometimes I fly, like a steel
needle, through air clean
and sharp as a cut, I feel
everything at once, I am elbow deep
in trees, their leaves caress
my face, and I can feel their roots
curl in the earth.
Sometimes I am too fast
for anyone to catch, I can do
and do more than I ever
could before. I go beyond
the need for sleep, inventing
unusual uses for every hour.
And sometimes I am far too tired
to be anyone, to walk or speak
or think. So I shut down
and send them all
home with a note
that I won't be back until the next
resurrection.

Things That Were Left Behind

Robert Hoffman

the antique amber ashtrays were stacked
here and there left outside to harden
and bake the burnt ashes of our all night
bull sessions at the trailer park playing
Hold 'Em until dawn in the midnight desert
heat collecting them like old tires and bones

the color of mother's coffee mug
the last thing she touched and drank from
with her lips that kissed you and told you
you were the best thing that ever happened
to her and I shared the same fate
we were her favorite because I was not

a momma's boy but I loved her anyway
three weeks after the half-filled cup had grown
moldy with the thick green memory
of her last sip and breath I couldn't bear
the sight of it over-growing and taking over
the trailer in a yeast darkness I washed the cup

and you hated my intrusion hated my resemblance
to her and the happy times we played pool
and drank while momma stayed sober
and when I washed the cup it was the last straw
for you as that mold was the last living thing
that she had touched because you had died

but were still breathing though half a year
would pass before you joined her and now
here I am with a stack of amber antique ashtrays
unwilling to wash them because trapped inside
the black and grey ash of cigar and cigarette
are the atoms of your breaths together

Serena Solin

Disciplinary Sonnet

Always tissue boxes in rooms like these,
where I'm assessed and curtly approved of,
referred, deferred to. Procedure swiftly
eclipses fear. When the hour's over
I run from the office like hair let down
stairs to street. I'm lighter. I cast off
didactic little sneers, idioms. Still,
violence liberated and well within,
lathering up to wellspring. When will I
open my hand, let the glass clutched in it
clatter to the ground? How will I then
be supported? I recognize the weight
that lifts when she asks me if I've ever
thought about hurting another person.

Ricardo Vidana
Out of the Blue

Ola Faleti

Panic

>I could
>have run
>into the slee-
>py midwestern
>street screaming I
>was going to die. I could
>have drafted my will. I could
>have called my mother. To tell her I
>love her. To let her hear my voice unhinge.
>I could have taken a shower. I could have ripped
>the posters off my walls after their faces grew callous,
>squirming and snatching up breath. I could have done anything to
>halt the reel in my head: bludgeoned sewer rats, floor crawling with roaches, my very flesh
>
>molting. I curled embryo-tight and shook instead.

Compilation

When she gets depressed she feels like an ogre standing outside a locked oak door to a tiny room filled with elves.

When he gets depressed he feels like burning everything down and then just leaving on a tramp steamer. But the men on board are even angrier than he is, so he wants to jump off the boat and go home, but he can't. Because he's on a fucking boat.

When she gets trauma triggered, she feels the eyes in the mask of the Bart Simpson character boring into her. They are big and staring and she can't tell who is real and who is a cartoon. It's a screen memory for some ancient event. But what?

They buy a gun when the cocaine wears off—which it always does—because they can't stand the world as it is.

When he gets depressed he writes a letter to God with a red sharpie.

When we get depressed we play online chess for hours and chat online with out of work (and therefore depressed) rabbis about the Talmud.

When she gets triggered she falls down a flight of stairs or cuts herself on accident. It hurts but it's good to feel *something*.

We watch TV. *Battlestar Gallactica* is particularly good. Except for the last season, which is stupid.

He reads complicated, out of date books.

When she gets triggered she tries to talk about it, but there are no words because whatever happened happened so long ago she can't remember it, but only feels it in her body and in her many phobias.

The people with the gun are clever and smart and they make her feel better. But then they use the gun.

Driving. Heights. Bees. The dark.

When she gets triggered she gets really angry and has to show people who's the boss. This scares people and they retreat. Then she gets really angry. It's a vicious circle. That depresses her.

When he gets depressed he can't get out of bed.

When she gets depressed she can't get to sleep.

Their funeral triggers a horror slide show that runs through her brain like an endless iphoto loop of outtakes from *Pan's Labyrinth*.

We write. We talk to the neighbors. We pull weeds. We go on walks. We read more books.

She watches her intake of alcohol.

He makes friends with the barista at Starbucks.

We do not buy a gun.

Roopa Dudley
Crypto Knight's Trophy

Kevin Ridgeway

Fleshy Mitten Jitters

My fingers are invisible at the rate they're traveling at, and I usually miscalculate when I attempt to applaud with the hands they sprouted from. When trying to give someone a High Five, I usually miss, slapping them in the face. It's not all clumsiness, it's neurons colliding inside my scratched phonograph record brain, my lithium salted nervous system not responding when I want to reach out to touch something or someone, and the flutter of this defective pair of butterfly claws always turns me into a wounded beast that cannot learn to hold on without breaking from the unwieldy curse of a low budget horror movie tremor that purrs wearily inside the rapid beat of its wrists.

Brandon Dumais

Survivor's Guilt

Kate pulled up her corduroy shorts
as we sat on the bleachers at Holyfield Park,
exposing the swells of red scars she made
with an X-acto blade along her smooth,
white thighs. I rolled my sleeves and pointed
at the faded marks I carved along my arms
with my pocket knife.

And then we fell in love.

We were nearing graduation and had big
embarrassing plans we could only tell
each other.
Kate wanted to die after the holidays.
I hadn't set a date.

The new year came. Kate got meds
and I had her, so our plans fell through
and we had to make new ones.
Then Kate got better and untied the trauma
that bonded us at the wrists, leaving
me with the slack to trip on as I continue
to think about her and our old plans
and how I never set a date.

Some days I wonder if she's ever felt survivor's guilt,
and then I remember I'm still alive.

Steve Lossing
Tex

Ed Baines *Ascending Descent*

Lynne Viti
Floor

Every day for years she has swallowed
the selective serotonin reuptake inhibitors.
They don't make me feel happy, she said,
but at least I can get up and put
one foot in front of the other.
The Zoloft creates a floor,
beneath which I know I won't fall. That's
the best it can do.

Walking, I think of this, this floor,
make my way along the bayside beach.
Ice chunks next to rushes
whipped, and beaten by early winter winds.
A thick layer of pine straw pads the walking trails.
I step lightly around a wire rectangle covering
beach hay, marked with a small blue flag
warning me off a turtle nest.

Down the empty main street in town, shops closed up
for the season, remnants of wreaths
stuck to the doors. No one inside.
Library, toy store, restaurants shuttered.
Only the market and the library interested in commerce,
winter vegetables, books and DVDs.
The solar panels of a house across the way
catch sunlight, grids glinting.
I recall the ground I knelt on yesterday when
I cut down dried miscanthus grasses
tied them with twine, stacked them in the garage. Solid
ground lets me kneel, sit, tread on it. The ground
is the floor below which I do not fall,
allows me to awaken,
put one foot in front of the other,
into the work. All this
holds me up, binds winter body to winter soul.

Aja Beech
Lady Lazarus Revisited

This earth refuses to
swallow me yet,
it spits me back out

each time, because
it needs me. Desperately.
More than I need the dark

soft soil to surround me,
more than I need the
worms as company.

And not just those times
I hung a looped belt
from a doorway,

and not just those times
I would smash my head
against tiled floors until unconscious.

It is also the time I ended
up in a car windshield
and walked away.

Or the time my face
met with the wrong end
of a cleated foot

splitting my head open
just at my left eyebrow.
I was awake

when the doctors sewed me
back up. I was awake
each time.

Time and again I think
If not now, when?
They Say: Not today, not today.

Kara Dennison

Ankle-Deep

I'm ankle-deep in blue-black water. I just dyed my hair again recently, black with blue streaks. The shower drain is never not clogged. I've tried every brand of clog remover. Nothing works. I don't like it. I never know if the tub will have drained enough for me to take an impromptu shower after a bad day or a sudden downpour. It's embarrassing for friends who stay more than a few days and need to shower. But I've adapted.

Whenever a friend makes a long-term visit, I give it a plunge or a pour of something "extra strength." It drains for a day or two. Then I'm ankle-deep in water again. I adapt. I make excuses if company has to deal with it.

Mazz comes to visit. She's understanding. But when I visited her in Carshalton, their shower drained perfectly. She's understanding. I'm embarrassed.

Two friends have just informed me one after the other that I'm "not myself." One feels helpless and angry because she wants to fix everything for me and she can't. The other feels helpless and frustrated because she's worried about me but I'm dropping the ball on things. Important things. Work things. I'm affecting others.

"Every problem you've had in my presence stems from the incorrect belief that you are not worthy of respect."

I agree with everything but the "incorrect." I don't remind her of the time my entire high school of 200 students bullied me out of school for something I didn't do. I don't remind her of the time an employer tricked me into scouting my own replacement. I don't remind her of the boyfriend who told me he was the only one who would ever love me because epilepsy and neglect left me too broken for anyone else to deal with. I don't remind her of the voice in the back of my head that tells me on a constant loop that any kindness done to me is a favor that I have to repay in kind, a goodwill gesture for a sad case.

"You need therapy. My husband got grief counseling. You saw how it changed him."

What would they do? Sit there and word-game me into accidentally admitting I'm important? I'm the queen of word-gaming.

I want a shower.

I don't want to be ankle-deep in water.

There's a cheerfully narrated YouTube video for "all you girls who don't want to hire a plumber." Pliers, coat hanger, flashlight. I have all of those. Let's go.

God, you could build an entire animal out of this. It's disgusting. It's fascinating. It's comforting. Now I can see what was down there. Now I know it's gone.

I have a shower. The water drains like it did in Carshalton. No cooling water pooling around my feet. I vanquished the big, disgusting thing making that happen.

So I wonder.

There's a counselor literally around the corner from me who takes my insurance.

I wonder.

The Perseids

Like the man behind the curtain, pulling levers, flipping switches, he controls the meteor showers. In your room, in the night, he stands beside your bed, draws you out of dream. Here is the creator of sky streaks, anxious to show his new work to a lucid you. Now on your patio still in the chill of an August night you stand barefoot, toes digging into stone, grinding skin, grounding self. You, the living, a rapt and willing audience. You, fully awake, fully aware, speak to the sky in its blackness and ask, childlike, to see this new secret. *Show me*, you say. *Prove you*. And there it is, streak of meteor, and then another. Bone, sinew, skin: fragments of light manifested in the sky. Home of loved soul: comet dust and fire.

Kim Sharp

Reasons to Worship the Moon

You may grow slow like a quartz crystal but you are magic and you heal. If you look within, you will find rainbows hidden inside. Like the Moon, you are covered in scars from all the wars you have fought to stay in orbit. You did it. You handled the asteroids and their hits. And you are still beautiful. You still light the sky. It's okay to wax and wane, to lose your shine for a night. Know it will come back. You will glow again and the moths and waves will crave you because there would be no ocean or places to build cocoons without you. Saturn may be surrounded by millions of moons but not one in that ring is you.

Amanda Martin

Kit Courter *Wind Turbine Study #27, Oak Creek Pass, CA*

Joy Shannon *Woman Contained #1*